Bee counts to ten:
"1, 2, 3, 4, 5, 6, 7, 8, 9, 10."

Then she starts to look for Snake.
Snake has hidden.

Is he in the sandbox?
Bee looks under the bucket...

Not there.

Is he up the tree?
Bee flies up and looks
at the tree top...

Not there.

Is he on top of the shed?
Bee looks on the roof...

Not there.

Is he under the shed?
Bee looks in the darkness
under the shed...

Not there.

Bee lands on the ground
and looks around.

Snake has hidden in a pot.
He peeks out to look for Bee.

Bee is still looking around.
Snake pops back and keeps still.

Bee looks.
"Was that a flash of red?" she thinks.

Snake keeps as still
as he can in the pot.

Then he peeps up
from the pot again.

"There you are!" cries
Bee, pointing to Snake.
"Found you!"